WalK liKe a WhiTe MaN™

Walk liKe a WhiTe MaN™

A Guide to Empowering Women
to Walk with Confidence and Boldness

Jeanita Jinnah

Nayla Book Publishers
Michigan

Nayla Book Publishers

P.O. Box 80714

Lansing, MI 48908

Walk Like a White Man™

Copyright © 2018 by Jeanita Jinnah

Cover Art by Darryl Anderson

All rights reserved.

No part of this book may be reproduced, scanned, or distributed in any printed or electronic form without permission. Please do not participate in or encourage piracy of copyrighted materials in violation of the author's rights. Purchase only authorized editions.

Paperback ISBN: 978-0-9863889-6-5

eBook ISBN: 978-0-9863889-7-2

This book is dedicated to:

- Anyone who has ever felt marginalized or has had certain labels placed on them.

- The person who has ever experienced the sting of the bully's whip.

- The little boy who was told he would never amount to anything.

- The little girl who was told she couldn't be something, or do something, because she is a girl.

- The wife who has become small and broken in her abusive marriage.

- The husband who has felt berated and belittled because he doesn't live up to his wife's standards of perfection.

- The person with disabilities who has been passed over for opportunities, jobs, housing, or even love because people see you as less than because of your disability.

Contents

Dedication - v

Introduction - ix

Walk Like a White Man - 15

Walk Like You Have Your Wallet in Your Back Pocket and You're Not Afraid - 21

Walk Like You've Never Been Followed Around in a Store - 29

Walk Like You've Never Had a White Woman Clutch Her Purse Close to Her when You Walk By - 35

Walk Like No One Has Ever Quickly Locked Their Car Doors When You Walked By - 39

Walk Like at any Moment Someone Might Walk

Up to You and Call You 'Master.' - 43

Walk Like You've Never Been Afraid to be Pulled Over by the Police - 49

If Your Presence Strikes Fear in the Heart of White People, It's Not Your Fault - 57

Do You Have to be White to Walk Like a White Man? - 61

Walk Like a White Man - Practice Exercises - 65

Walk Like a White Man – Spotlight - 73

Walk Like a White Man – Quotes - 95

Epilogue - 99

Introduction

I decided to write this book for all the people who have ever felt marginalized, had their rights taken away unjustly, or felt powerless. Today is the day that you take your power back.

Walk Like a White Man™ is an inspirational book and online community where women come together to uplift and to be uplifted. We've discovered the secret to success and achieving your goals. Finding the internal strength that's already in you naturally, believing in that strength, and activating it with measured and calculated action plans focused on a specific goal; we call this, your internal powers, your Super Girl Powers.

Super Girl Powers are powers you may not have known you had until you discovered them while going through difficult times. They were always there, but because you were not aware of them, and therefore never activated them, they remained dormant in your life until you urgently needed them.

I discovered my Super Girl Power after having gone through grief and depression after losing my husband of seven years to cancer. I never knew how strong I was until I went through this experience. Until I had to rely on an internal power that helped boost me out of grief and depression. What's my Super Girl Power? My Super Girl Power is quiet strength. This strength that lived dormant inside me for years became visible, not in a forceful way, but in a quiet determined way. It was persistent in its will to survive. But not just survive. Thrive. And even though it has been a long and tedious process, my quiet strength would not relent in getting me to embrace my strength, and my will to live.

It's important to understand your strengths so that you can put them to use to be a force for good. Too many people are walking around today with their God-given power having been taken away from them. Someone told you that you were weak and you believed them. And because you believed them, you started behaving like you were weak. And the more you acted weak the weaker you became. Well not anymore. Not after today.

Now that you know that you have this strength inside you, you will start looking for it. You will expect it to work for you. When you feel you have lost all strength and feel you can't go on, something inside you will tell you, "You must go on." Something inside you will push you forward. Something inside you will not let you die.

As an observer of people, I believe that certain people, based on various factors such as race, class, gender, and socioeconomic status have a particular way of moving around on the earth. Their background, upbringing, and training have developed in them certain beliefs about their lot in life, where they belong in society, and how people should treat them.

Take for example, white men. I've noticed that white men usually carry themselves in more confident and assertive ways. This confidence is based on many things, some of which we will look at in this book.

If you get nothing else from this book, I hope you walk away with a deeper understanding of your internal strengths, and how to utilize these strengths to help you get through difficult situations. And I hope you learn to utilize the power of visually stimulating reference material, if you need it, to help you achieve what you want to achieve in life.

After reading this book, and getting a mental picture of why many white men are able to succeed in life where others may fail, I hope you can use this as a visual stimulant to help you set and achieve your goals.

Walk Like a White Man

Have you ever noticed how white men walk around in the world? Confidently. Head up. Shoulders back. Looking straight ahead. White men don't really take much notice of who's walking around them. They are focused on where they want to go, and moving forward in order to get there.

White men have been raised from little boys to believe that they are important. That they can do anything they set their minds to, and be anything they want to be. These beliefs have been instilled in them early on. White men are taught as little boys that they have a place in this world. That they can conquer the world. And, in some cases, that the world can become their oyster.

Because of these attitudes being instilled in them, white men feel confident about their place in the world. They feel they have an important role to play. Not just in the world, also in their family, in their schools, in their community, and in the civic discourse taking place around them. White men feel they belong in all of these venues and look at what they see as their God-given responsibility with pride.

For this reason, you will rarely see a white man with his head hung down. You will rarely see a white man looking defeated or seeming dejected. You will rarely see a white man's shoulders sagging like the burden he has to carry is too heavy for him to bear. This just doesn't happen in a white man's world. Because to a white man, he is the master of his own universe.

It's for this reason that I think *everyone* should walk like a white man. Everyone should walk confidently through life feeling like he or she matters. Everyone should walk boldly and confidently, without quaking or fear, into their destiny – the destiny that has been determined for you before you were born.

This book gives you, no matter who you are, permission to walk like a white man. It encourages you to walk boldly and confidently about in your world, and the world around you. It teaches you how to live your life like you were at the top of the food chain. Like a lion - king of the jungle.

Walk Like A White Man™ takes an introspective, yet quirky, approach to what it's like to be a white man. The theme of this book is one of inspiration and motivation. I try to keep it fun, upbeat, and positive, while being very much aware of the underlying tension that might go along with a book with a title like *Walk Like A White Man*™. It is never my intention to suggest or even imply that everyone should seek to be white, or better yet, deny who you are. I simply seek to encourage you to be who you are, the way God made you, yet elevate your way of thinking and raise the level of your consciousness as a way of fostering pride and confidence in yourself. Bottom line, *Walk Like A White Man*™ is a book about confidence, self-assuredness, pride, and owning your space. It's also about not letting others define who you are. This is your job, and your job alone.

Included in this book are *Walk Like A White Man*™ *Practices Exercises*, to help you gain confidence with visually stimulating references to keep you motivated. Also included is a *Walk Like A White Man*™ *Spotlight*, where we look at individuals, of various races, and genders, who practiced walking like a white man in some form, who you can gain inspiration from. And finally, *Walk Like A White Man*™ *Quotes* to help highlight some of the inspirational material in the book you have read. These quotes are meant to be "carry-alongs" that you can take with you on your journey of confidence and self-assuredness.

So, are you ready? Let's get to it!

Walk Like You Have Your Wallet in Your Back Pocket and You're Not Afraid

Men tend to carry everything they own in their pockets, unlike women, who carry their belongings in their purse, slung over their shoulder. Women carry purses because generally pockets aren't standard on most women's clothing. You will however find some pockets on women's pants and jeans, and even some shirts. These are pretty much typical. But designers usually don't put many pockets on women's skirts, blouses, and blazers. Not functional pockets anyway. Pockets tend to add unwanted bulk for women. But for men's clothing, pockets are essential. And the more pockets the better.

It's normal to see men carry their wallet in their back pocket. And now that I think about it, it's usually always their right back pocket. I don't think I've ever seen a man carry his wallet in is left back pocket. You might argue that if a man is right-handed it's more natural for him to reach back with his right hand into his right back pocket. But, I know men who are left-handed, and they still carry their wallet in their right back pocket. This seems to be pretty common for men. Maybe this stems back to when these men were little boys and they would watch their dads getting dressed in the morning, and this is where they saw dad place his wallet. We tend to imitate what we see as children. And these things tend to follow us into adulthood.

Anyway, I digress... What were we talking about? Oh yeah, white men.

I guess I'll never really know what it's like to be a white man, because I'm not a white man. But what I am is an honest observer. I watch people. I study their habits and mannerisms. And I listen to them speak. And more importantly, I listen to what they *don't* say. I've found from studying people that you can learn a lot about them from what they *don't* say. And while white men don't always openly speak what they're thinking (most men don't), the way they carry themselves, and the way they move around in the world speaks volumes about who they are.

We were talking just a moment ago about men carrying their wallet in their back pocket. I point this out because people are most vulnerable from behind. Because, naturally, we don't have eyes in the back of our head we don't really know what's going on behind us. Think about it. We often hear about people being "stabbed in the back" by someone they thought was their friend. This is a big deal because you expect your friend to have your back – your most vulnerable side. So when someone you trust stabs you in the back, not only do you not see it coming, but your guard is down because this was your friend. And no one would expect a friend to stab them in the back.

Our vulnerabilities are often exposed and sometimes exploited by those we call 'friend.' We often carry these people around in our "back pocket." They are the people we love and cherish the most. So not only is our wallet in our back pocket, our livelihood is also in our back pocket. Our hopes and dreams are often also in our back pocket. And those treasures we hold dear are in our back pocket.

Being vulnerable is sometimes the hardest thing we can do. To us vulnerability may expose our weaknesses. And no one wants to appear weak. Everyone wants to put out an image of strength to the world. But the truth of the matter is that we all have weaknesses that can be exploited at any given time. A woman may be vulnerable to controlling and manipulative men. Maybe as a little girl she saw her mom being controlled by her dad, and this became normal to her. Or perhaps a man may be vulnerable to manipulative and cunning women who are only out to use him and take all they can get from him. Thinking that these women really care about him, and feeling he can handle himself, this man opens himself up to greater manipulation the more he releases power and control to these manipulative women.

No one wants to appear vulnerable. But the truth is that when you "place your wallet in your back pocket," you are vulnerable. When you place too much blind trust in people, even those who call themselves your friends, you are vulnerable. And anytime you open your heart up to someone for love, you are vulnerable.

So what do you do? Do you stop trusting people? Do you think that everybody is out to get you? Do you move to an island and remove yourself from society, hoping that not being around people will make you less vulnerable? No, all this does is isolate you. Solitude is probably one of the worst things you can do to a person. We are meant to be social beings. After an extended period of time in solitude, you'll find yourself going "crazy." You can only talk to yourself for so long before you feel you *are* crazy. Human contact is natural and it stimulates all of our senses. So no, the answer is not to wall yourself off from people. People who do this usually become bitter people. They begin to slowly die inside, whether they know it or not, from lack of substantive human contact. It's almost like lonely people begin to decay inside from extended periods of isolation. I'm sure you know someone, or have heard of someone, like this. Some of these people are not pleasant to be around. It's like a dark cloud follows them around everywhere they go, and if you get too close to them you will also be engulfed in the dark cloud.

We are made to love. To be happy. To give. To share. To care. This is normal for us. The people who fight against this are the ones who have chosen another path in life. Some people like to surround themselves with darkness. I refuse to walk in that darkness.

Walk Like You've Never Been Followed Around in a Store

If you are a person of color, you've probably experienced the humiliation of being followed around in a store. And the reason you are watched and followed so closely is because someone has made up his or her mind, just by looking at you, that you are probably a thief, and will probably steal something from their store if they don't keep a close eye on you.

Why people automatically jump to these conclusions is beyond me. But we all have certain prejudices embedded in us based on our upbringing, our fears, the movies and television shows we watch, our perceptions, or misconceptions, and of course, ignorance – which is often willful. All of us have at some point formed certain biases about a certain group of people based on what's going on in our own hearts and minds. It may have nothing to do with the people we've formed prejudices about but we make it about them just the same.

Usually what's going on inside us is projected on other people. Do you see this? When someone says something out of the way or derogatory about me, I think to myself, "That has nothing to do with me." And it usually doesn't. I know that the person's comment has nothing to do with me, or who I am. It's usually more about the person making the comment. They are the ones who have the problem. Not me.

So when I get followed around in a store for

no good reason, I know that this person's thinking in their mind that I am a thief has nothing to do with me. Why? It has nothing to do with me because I've never stolen anything before in my life. Not even a pack of gum. That's just not who I am, and it's not how I was raised. I am not a thief, and I will not, and have never stolen anything out of a store. So that's why I say I'm not the person with the problem. The person making the bigoted, prejudiced assumption about me has the problem. I think if more people understood this, it would free them from carrying around anger and bitterness from others placing these unjustified labels on them.

White men don't know how it feels to be followed around in a store, or accused presumptuously of being a thief based simply on some bigoted perceptions that their ignorant accusers have of them.

When a white man walks into a store, he

walks in free of the burden of ever being accused of being a thief. He never feels accusatory eyes on him while he's browsing the aisles searching for the item he came in to purchase. White men are usually given the benefit of the doubt, that they will pay for what they want, and not just take it. And, that they can *afford* to pay for it. A white man's burdens are different from a black man's, a Hispanic man's, an Asian man's, etc. I'm not saying white men don't have burdens, they just have different burdens.

When have you heard a white man say he feels he's being treated unfairly because people just automatically assumes he is a thief when he walks into their store? How many white men have you seen being followed around in a store? If anything, the clerk or shop owner welcomes his white customer into his shop gladly. Greets him warmly. And goes out of his way to help him. This is how many white people are treated in stores, and this is quite normal to them. So normal, in fact, that they can't imagine being treated any other way, nor can they relate when someone, who is not white, says they have a different experience. *Well, why would your experience be different from mine?* They just don't get it.

Walk Like You've Never Had a White Woman Clutch Her Purse Close to Her when You Walk By

Oh dear. Has this ever happened to you? You're walking through the store minding your business when you notice a white woman with her purse sitting in the shopping cart unattended. Incidentally, I've never understood this. Why would any woman leave her purse unattended - especially in the times we're living in? But it happens every day. And the fear that strikes a white woman when a black person (man or woman) walks by happens more often than you'd like to think.

Where do these ideas come from? Why is there an instant trigger of fear inside a white woman when a black man, or woman, walks by? Black people have been given boogey man status in some homes and cultures. And it can't help that there are often negative and stereotypical betrayals of black men on TV. These negative portrayals have been going on for many years. Black men are often picked to play the villain. The gangster. The thug. This is not representative of all black men, and you're starting to see more positive roles for blacks on TV. But if the only contact you have with black men is through your television screen it's no wonder black men are labeled, and their very presence strikes fear in the hearts of white women.

I think the more we get acquainted with people and get to know them personally these stereotypes will become less engrained in our minds and hearts. Hang around black people and people of color and get to know them – as human beings with the same or similar hopes and dreams that you have for yourself and your family. We are all God's creatures, and made in His image. Therefore, there is good (and bad) in all of us. The bad doesn't come from God. It comes from fallen man. We have Adam and Eve to blame for this. (Thanks guys!)

I'm pretty sure white men as a whole don't walk around in fear of being labeled a thief. Or perceived to be a purse snatcher. White women don't appear to have the same uneasiness inside when a white man walks by. They don't experience their heart beat pick up, or cold sweats break out when a white man walks by. I've said it before and I'll say it again, get to know the people of color around you. Start with the people in your neighborhood. Just randomly and unprovoked strike up a conversation with a person of color. This is one way to minimize fear — by confronting it and putting it to rest. Trust me, fear is nothing we should want to live with. Fear is constricting and binding. Freedom is what you should desire. Freedom from the bondage of negative stereotypes that rob you of your life, and keep you from experiencing pure joy.

Walk like a white man who's never been perceived to be a purse snatcher, even if you have. Don't let these false narratives define you. Just remember: "That has nothing to do with me." Repeat this a few times until it begins to sink in: "That has nothing to do with me."

Walk Like No One Has Ever Quickly Locked Their Car Doors When You Walked By

Here's another thing that many people of color have experienced. You're out for a walk when you suddenly come to an intersection, and you notice the woman sitting in a car at the stop light quickly lock her car door. Today, power locks come standard in most cars, so people can get away with locking their car doors without being too obvious. But back in the day, before power locks, people had to manually lock their car doors. And if this has ever happened to you, you never forget it. And with that quick motion of reaching over and locking her door this lady has just painted you with a broad stroke, and labeled you a person who might possibly do her harm.

Do we really not think about how our actions, which are based on prejudices and irrational fear, make other people feel? Do we not see it? Do we not get it? I know it's hard to put ourselves into someone else's shoes, but sometimes we need to. Put yourself in the shoes of the person standing on the corner waiting for the light to change when suddenly they see someone in the car waiting at the light quickly reach over and lock her car door. How would that make you feel? How would you react? How *should* you react? I think it's safe to say that it wouldn't make you feel good. It might actually make you feel mad. Mad at being made to be something you're not. Mad at how certain people think that it's okay to treat people the way they themselves wouldn't want to be treated. And mad at the unfairness of it all.

But, the reality is, in spite of all this, we can't walk around in a perpetual state of "mad." Yes, there is unfairness in life. Yes, we will sometimes be subjected to prejudice and bigotry. And yes, life will sometimes be unkind. But how you handle all of this is the key. And frankly, I think we have enough people walking around mad. I'm almost certain that some people wake up every morning, look in the mirror, and they become mad. I bet you didn't know this, did you? Some people wake up mad. Unfortunately, we have to live around these people every day. Mad people are unpleasant to be around. And I try and stay as far away from these people as humanly possible. I wouldn't want this disease to rub off on me. The "mad disease." Now is that the same thing as the mad cow disease? Never mind...

Bottom line: Walk like you have nothing to fear. Walk like you own your space. Walk with your shoulders back, and your head up. Walk like a white man.

Walk Like at any Moment Someone Might Walk Up to You and Call You 'Master.'

What?! I can't believe you went there! Oh yes I did. I'm going there. In my observations, some men seem to have a "master" complex. For some reason, they like to walk around calling themselves master. What is this all about? Where does this stem from? No matter what arena in life, and no matter what station. Whenever men want to put out the image that they've achieved a certain status in life, or in their career, they tend to tack the word "Master" onto their title. For example, Master Carpenter, Master Journeyman, Master Builder, Master Copywriter. Master. Master. Master. Men seem to love this word! I don't think I've heard of too many women calling themselves 'master.' Master Mom (umm... I don't think so). Master Chef (oh wait, <u>men</u> have already taken over that title). Master Seamstress (nope...). Master CEO (now that just sounds weird). Yeah, I think it's safe to say that men have taken over the "Master" title. Women, I suspect, don't feel they need to take on such a title. They just *are.* They just *do.* They just *be.* No titles required.

The "master" complex is a perplexing one to me. Someone will have to explain this one to me. Nevertheless, it's very real. And from my observations white men tend to have this complex more often than most. Although, other men from other races may be tapping into it more. The one standout to me is when people in America held individuals in slavery against their will. People owned people just like you would own a piece of land or livestock. And the white slave owners were big on having their slaves call them "Master." Master John. Master Ed. Master Tom. These white men surely loved the sound of the word.

I can imagine being called master gave these slave owners a sense of pride, or a sense of importance. It must have elevated their status in the community. "Do you know that Robert over in Adams County owns about 12 slaves?" "Oh, really?" "Yes, he does. He's doing quite well for himself." Back then, people aspired to acquire land and a few slaves so they could prosper and have status in the community. And the poor slaves, well, they just had to endure being treated as property, and being used for free labor. I'm sure many, if not all, resented these white men who owned and sold them like cattle. Thankfully, this type of system doesn't exist in this country anymore. But men have found a new way to get this same type of fulfillment and stature by calling themselves master. Master of their specific craft.

Imagine being a white man who had people running behind him calling him "Master." How might this man have walked? Probably with an air of importance. A sense of purpose. A feeling of pride. There must have been an invisible string that descended from the clouds, and attached itself to his chin, and held his head up high when he walked. Or what about the bellows that lived inside his chest, along with the little servant gnome who pumped air into the bellows which subsequently supplied air to the white man's chest, which would rise and contract with every pump of the bellows made by the servant gnome. The white man's chest must have filled up with pride every time he heard the word "Master."

Imagine this white man's walk. He must have felt as light as a balloon with every step he took. Walk like this white man. Walk like gravity is your friend. Walk like you are the master of your universe. Walk like at any moment someone might run up to you and call you master. Walk like a white man.

Walk Like You've Never Been Afraid to be Pulled Over by the Police

You would have to be living under a rock to have not heard people of color complain about being harassed by the police. People of color in general have vastly different experiences with police officers. The police are supposed to be a most trusted ally in the community. You are supposed to feel safe when you see the police ride through your neighborhood. You are not supposed to break into a cold sweat when you see the flashing lights of a police car in your rearview mirror. You should feel comfortable chumming around with the police officers assigned to patrol your neighborhood. You should, but most people in this country, unfortunately, do not feel a sense of goodwill and light-hearted regard for police officers. It all depends on your experiences, and the experiences of the group of people you belong to. If you've had only good experiences then it's only natural for you to feel safe around the police. But if your experiences have not been so good, you're going to naturally view the police with a wary eye, and a high sense of concern. Everyone has their perception of police officers, based on their own experiences.

Listen to the average white man speak about police officers and you will see that he usually has such high regard for them; but if you listen to the average black man speak, he usually doesn't view the police with such high regard. Experience and proximity to the particular demographic group based on these experiences is key.

According to a 2015 Gallup poll, in the U.S., confidence in police is at the lowest that it has been in 22 years, at 52%. Confidence has ranged fairly narrowly between 52% and 64% since 1993.

Americans' Confidence in the Police

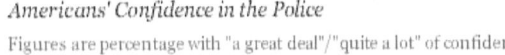

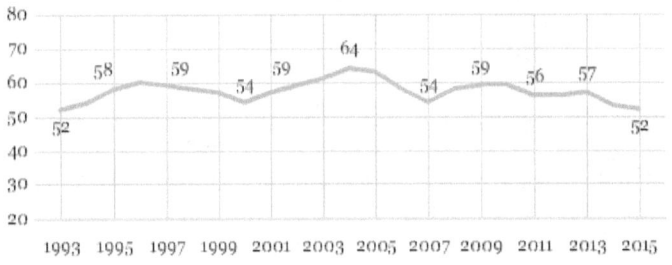

GALLUP

Overall, 25% of Americans say they have a great deal of confidence in the police, 27% quite a lot, 30% "some," 16% "very little" and 2% "none." The combined 18% who have very little or no confidence in police is the highest Gallup has measured to date.

(Gallup poll)

According to the 2015 Gallup poll, Democrats show the largest loss of confidence in police. Democrats (42%) now have less confidence in police than independents (51%) and remain much less confident than Republicans (69%).

By demographics, police confidence in 2015 is White (57%), Nonwhite (42%), Black (30%), and Hispanic (52%). There are many factors to account for these numbers. Again, if you've ever had a negative experience with the police you will more naturally feel more wary of the police. But if your experiences have been mostly positive then you will quite naturally feel positively about the police.

I remember shortly after George Zimmerman was acquitted of killing Trayvon Martin we witnessed an incident caught on camera where George was pulled over by a police officer in Texas for speeding. George Zimmerman was the neighborhood watch captain in Ferguson, Missouri who was charged and acquitted of killing an unarmed black youth (Trayvon Martin) who was walking home from his neighborhood store.

Luckily, there was a dash cam in the officer's patrol car to record the traffic stop. When the police officer approached Mr. Zimmerman's truck he was clearly nervous. The officer had to tell him to calm down. During the traffic stop, Mr. Zimmerman informed the police officer that he had a gun in the glove box and opened the glove box to reveal the firearm to the officer. The officer took Mr. Zimmerman's license and registration and told him to close the glove box and not "play with his firearm," and proceeded to turn his back on Mr. Zimmerman and walk back to his patrol car. My initial reaction was shock when I saw the recorded footage of this. First of all, I thought, now if that had been a black man, or a Hispanic man, he would have been snatched out of the truck and put in handcuffs "for your safety and mine." But this didn't happen to Mr. Zimmerman, who is a white man. He was given the benefit of the doubt and told to stay calm and not play with his firearm while the officer walked back to his patrol car to check Mr. Zimmerman's record. Am I the only one shocked by this? Maybe I've seen too many incidents of black men coming in contact with the police and it going very differently, and I'm sure you have too. Nevertheless, this is one incident that shows us why your impression of the police might be different based on your circumstances and experiences.

I'm sure it's safe to say that Mr. Zimmerman was glad to be a white man on this day, otherwise we could have witnessed an entirely different encounter.

Whether you are a black man, a white man, a Hispanic man, or an Asian man just know that you all have a place in this world. You have a right to feel safe. And you should feel that the Constitution of the United States applies to you, and ensures you certain liberties and rights as citizens. In this you should feel confident.

Don't allow negative stereotypes to change who you are, or to cause you to become bitter. And don't let someone's negative perception of you become the perception you have of yourself. In other words, don't internalize someone else's views of you. Be your own person. Own your own space. And live your life with confidence, and be confident in the rights and liberties afforded you by the Constitution. Yes, even you have the right to life, liberty, and the pursuit of happiness. Hold your head up high and walk with confidence in knowing that the Constitution supports your right to exist. Walk like a white man.

If Your Presence Strikes Fear in the Heart of White People, It's Not Your Fault

I was out for a walk one afternoon when I spotted a white lady and her dog walking on the sidewalk toward me. Now, whenever I see a person walking his or her dog with one of those long, retractable leashes where the dog is practically walking himself, I know that the owner doesn't have full control over his or her dog. And I usually, quietly and politely, cross the street to the other side to let them and their dog have the sidewalk. I especially do this when I see the dog on high alert, and the owner distracted, or acting nonchalant. This is what happened on this particular day. I crossed to the middle of the street to where there was a grassy island, and walked near the island in the street until I had passed the lady and her dog. Walking along the grassy part of the island was a lone goose, squawking and making a lot of noise. The dog started barking and suddenly lunged toward me while his owner tried hard to contain him (this is why I removed myself from the sidewalk and crossed the street). Suddenly, the squawking goose flew away. When this happened, the lady holding the dog said, "Oh, I thought he was lunging at you." She assumed her dog was lunging at the goose. I said nothing, I just kept walking.

I knew that there was a 50/50 chance the dog was lunging at me and not the goose. Dogs are really sensitive to what their owners are feeling at the time. And if the owner tenses up when she sees a person walking towards them, the dog's going to pick up on this and, naturally, try and protect his owner, because the owner's feeling weak and vulnerable. That's probably what was happening with this dog. He sensed his owner's fear, or apprehension, and lunged at either the goose, or me, in a protective manner.

Fearful people are walking around with a loaded weapon on the end of a leash – their dogs. Everyone is in danger of a fearful person, because they are so unpredictable. Fear makes one act irrationally. You may feel that someone is trying to harm you even though they're not.

On this day I was out for a walk enjoying the beautiful weather, minding my own business, when I encountered this lady and her over protective dog. This could have ended differently if I hadn't had the presence of mind to cross over to the other side of the street. This lady's fear, angst, apprehension…

whatever it was... on this day was not my fault. It was based on what was going on inside of her at the moment she spotted me walking on the sidewalk. I've told you before, that when people have these kinds of misconceptions about me I understand that it has nothing to do with me. Nothing to do with who I am. And nothing to do with anything I have done. I am just me. And if people have a problem with that, it's their fault, not mine.

Do not. I repeat, do not take these things personally. I know, it's hard not to, especially when it *is* personal. But again, repeat after me: "That has nothing to do with me."

Do You Have to be White to Walk Like a White Man?

So the question is, do you have to be white to walk like a white man? Absolutely not! Anyone can walk like a white man regardless of the color of his or her skin. Walking like a white man is not a cultural thing. It's an attitude. It's a belief. It's a mindset. When you walk like a white man you are saying that you are confident and strong. And you own your space. You walk into a store without fear of being prejudged. You walk into a room without fear of a white woman shrinking in fear. You carry yourself like you belong in this space, because no one's ever told you that you don't.

This book is not just a book for people of color. It's for anyone who has ever felt marginalized or penalized for being part of a group who has had certain labels placed on them for whatever reason. It's for the person who has ever felt belittled or put down. For the person who has ever experienced the sting of the bully's whip. This book is for the little boy who was told he would never amount to anything. And for the little girl who was told she couldn't be something, or do something, because she is a girl. This book is for the wife who has become small and broken in her abusive marriage. And for the husband who has felt berated and belittled because he doesn't live up to his wife's standards of perfection. And it's for the person with disabilities who has been passed over for opportunities, jobs, housing, or even love because people see you as less than because of your disability.

This book gives you permission to carry yourself with confidence and strength. It's your permission to see yourself as worthy and valuable. And it is your permission to step out of those confining labels and be who you were created to be. Live the life you were meant to live. And walk the path you were meant to walk without obstacles and roadblocks keeping you confined and stagnant.

Walk Like a White Man™ is like the coach in the room cheering you on and rooting for your success. *You are strong! You've got this! You can do it! Hold your head up! Keep trying!* It's like the loving parent trying to instill strength and confidence in her child. Or the teacher who sees something special in one of his students and tries really hard to bring it out. *Walk Like a White Man*™ is for you! It's for who you are, and who you can become. Don't let society's limited perspectives and perceptions define who you are, or dim your shine. Hold your head up. Square your shoulders. And walk confidently into your destiny. Walk like a white man who has nothing to fear.

Walk Like a White Man - Practice Exercises

1. If you start to see your shoulders sag, your back hunched, or your chest deflated picture yourself as the hero in a story who rides in on a beautiful white stallion to save the beautiful frightened woman from the big, ugly ogre who has kidnapped her and tied her up in his dark and dank secretive cabin hidden deep in the woods, away from civilization. You're the hero of this story, and this story was written just to showcase your heroism and your absence of fear in an otherwise frightening situation.

2. If you walk into a store and the store clerk is noticeably concerned about your presence in the store to the point where he starts to follow you around the store to "keep an eye on you," stop, turn around, look him square in the eye and say "Sir, is there a problem?" When he starts to turn red with embarrassment, and is confused at your confidence to point out his behavior, gently, and politely say "I noticed that you are following me around the store. Is there a problem?" When he denies that there is a "problem" politely say, "Okay, good. I'm glad we don't have a problem." Continue your shopping and go on your merry way. I guarantee you this shopkeeper will not forget you. I'm sure this is the first time someone has ever so boldly and confidently confronted him – pointing out his blatant prejudices. People usually back down when you call them out.

Or, you could do what I sometimes do when a store clerk follows me around the store, keeping a suspicious eye on me. Make them work for it! Here's what I mean. Maybe this is just the ornery side of me, but when I notice a clerk following closely behind me, and watching me like a hawk, I'll sometimes make giant zigzag patterns around the entire store, going from left to right, or right to left, then front to back, and back to front. If you're going to follow me, I'm going to make you work for your money. I hope you're wearing comfortable shoes! Might as well have a little fun – at the clerk's expense.

3. If you believe you are being singled out because of your race or gender or whatever, try not to take it personally. Or at least try and get over it quickly, because personalizing this will only harm you in the end. The person who has offended you is long gone and has probably thought no more about it. You, on the other hand, have carried your frustration and resentment at the person around like one carrying a dead man around on his back. This dead man, or in this case, anger and resentment, has begun to weigh you down, poison your soul, and left you feeling drained and less energetic. This... is... not... a... good... way... to... live. Let it go! Get the dead man off your back before he kills you. Remember, people carry around prejudice and bigotry based on who they are. It has nothing to do with you, or who you are. Why internalize someone else's problems? That's just like carrying a dead man around on your back. Eventually, he will kill you. What does this dead man mean to you? Nothing? Then let him go.

4. The next time you go for a job interview, instead of walking into the room feeling like a caged animal in the zoo who wants nothing more than to escape, walk in like the job is already yours, and you're just coming to get what belongs to you – your job! Walk into the room confidently, like you're the one running the meeting and thus setting the tone for the meeting. Ask your interviewer as many, or more, questions as he or she asks you. After all, you are also trying to determine if this job is the right fit for *you,* as much as the interviewer is sizing you up for the job. Don't walk into the room timid or apologetically, like you're interrupting them in some way. Walk in like you're rescuing the interviewer(s) from having to interview candidate after candidate hoping to stumble upon the right one. When they meet you, you will wow their socks off, make them feel comfortable, and make them ready to make you an offer right then and there. Walk into your next interview with confidence and self-assurance. Because if you believe it, the job is already yours.

5. The next time you're in the mall, notice how white men sometimes walk around in the mall. Have you noticed how some men like to spread themselves out like a peacock as they walk the aisles, taking up more than enough space, and expecting everyone to make the necessary adjustments to maneuver around them and avoid bumping into them? They've claimed their personal space (a large swath of area), and keep barreling ahead, therefore, making everyone else have to go around them, and adjust their gait and personal space to make way for Mr. Peacock. Some might call this a form of manspreading. Men have a tendency to claim their space, and sometimes some of your space too. The next time you're in the mall, don't be rude about it, just practice claiming your space. Don't walk with timidity, walk with confidence. Head up, shoulders back, and eyes focused on where you want to go. You might even nod and smile at people as you go by. This is not about claiming anyone else's space, but simply about claiming your space, or better yet, being confident in the space you're in. Try it. This is a great exercise to help you gain confidence, and walk in a more self-assured manner. Confidence. Confidence. Confidence. Never arrogance.

Walk Like A White Man – Spotlight

John Wayne

John Wayne, born Marion Robert Morrison, May 26, 1907 – June 11, 1979, was an American actor, also known as Duke. John was a man's man – rugged, strong, confident, the envy of men everywhere, and desired by women. Movie studios often cast him as the leading man in their films. John was always the last man standing. The fastest gunslinger in the West. The swash buckling hero who swept in to save vulnerable women from big, bad men. John Wayne was a legend. He received a hero's welcome everywhere he went. He was admired and celebrated. John's films were highly acclaimed, and received great praise. Fans loved him, and many wished they could be like him. To this day, there are still legions of adoring John Wayne fans who idolize their hero.

John walked onto a movie set, and into the lives of television audiences, with great confidence. He was confident in his ability to handle any situation, to gain respect from his friends and enemies alike. His walk wasn't so much a swagger as it was a long, tall stroll. You see, John stood 6 feet 4 inches tall. Yet, it was both his stature and commanding presence that got him attention when he walked. People stood up and took notice when John walked by. Not only was his height intoxicating, but his lingering aura drew people's attention as they became quickly aware of his presence. John was aware of what his commanding presence did to people when he walked into a room, and he came to embrace it. He wore every inch of his stature, poise, and mystique like a fitted suit tailor-made for its occupant.

Study John Wayne's walk. He walked like a white man well aware of his calling and purpose, and confident in his ability to fulfill it. This was a white man who truly owned his space. As I stated before, you don't need to be a white man to walk like a white man, as our next example points out, although John Wayne just happened to be a white man. Anyone, no matter who you are, and no matter how you've walked in the past, can learn to walk like a white man.

For more information on John Wayne, visit the official John Wayne website: https://johnwayne.com/.

Martin Luther King, Jr.

Have you ever been to the mountaintop and looked over? Do you know what it takes to make it to the mountaintop? Lots of grit, fortitude, unrelenting obstacles, and hard work.

Martin Luther King, Jr. (January 15, 1929 –

April 4, 1968), was an American Baptist minister, scholar, social activist, and civil rights leader. And after his assassination, he became a legend. When Martin Luther King was alive, to many, he was an agitator, a rabble rouser, an uppity black man, and an all-around troublemaker.

Martin was an African American man who was born and raised in the South. Around the time Martin rose to prominence, locally and eventually around the world, the South was known for its laws and attitudes that were not favorable to blacks. Black people could not vote, could not patronize certain stores and restaurants, could not sit where they wanted on public transportation, and could not attend certain schools. According to some in the South, black people were looked at as less than human, and certainly not equal to white folks.

But Martin Luther King had a calling, and a passion for justice and equality for everyone, regardless of the color of their skin. Having experienced the injustice and pain of segregation and the Jim Crow laws of the South, Martin was fed up enough with the injustice to speak up, to stand up, and to fight back. But Martin preached a message of non-violent resistance. Resistance to the unjust laws that kept blacks confined to second-class citizenry.

Martin dreamed of a day when all men, black and white, and brown and yellow would be treated as equals. A day when there would once and for all be an end to segregation and racism. A day when all of God's people would be treated as one. Martin carried himself as one who was assured of his God-given rights – to life, liberty, and the pursuit of happiness. He believed that his skin color did not make him less than, as some tried to make him believe. Martin was not afraid to assert his rights, even in the face of the threat of imprisonment, beatings, loss of freedom, and ultimately, death. He was assured of his rights and believed that one day he could persuade his enemies that he was not a threat to them, and that equal rights for all was not a threat to them. In fact, it would only make things better in the end, not just for blacks, but also for whites.

Martin Luther King was a confident man in the face of danger. And even though he was a black man living in the South, he eventually learned to carry himself as though he were a white man, with all the rights that the law, at that time, afforded to white men. He was a black man who walked like a white man. And he was determined to continue to walk like a white man until the antiquated and racially bigoted laws of the Jim Crow South finally caught up with who he believed himself to be, and encouraged other blacks, at the time, to also walk the walk and talk the talk. These blacks walked like white men before it was even popular to do so, and in spite of the danger to do so.

Harriet Tubman

Born into slavery in Maryland, Harriet Tubman (c. 1820 to March 10, 1913) escaped to freedom in the North in 1849 to become the most famous "conductor" on the Underground Railroad. Harriet Tubman, born Araminta Ross, "Minty", was an American abolitionist, humanitarian, and an armed scout and spy for the United States Army during the American Civil War. Araminta later adopted her mother's first name, Harriet. Tubman comes from her husband, John Tubman, a free black, whom she married in 1844.

From early childhood Harriet suffered from a debilitating head injury that caused dizziness, pain, seizures, and spells of hypersomnia caused by an irate slave owner throwing a heavy metal weight, intending to hit another slave, which hit Harriet in the head instead.

Life was hard for Harriet as a slave. She was often whipped and abused by abusive slave owners starting from early childhood. After she escaped to freedom to Philadelphia, and eventually settled in Canada for a time, and subsequently retired in New York in her later years, Harriet suffered from poverty, theft of her money by scammers, and the illnesses that rocked her from her time as a slave. Yet, Harriet did not let any of this stop her. She felt she had a calling from God, and was often called "Moses" after the prophet in the Bible whom God used to deliver Israel out of Egypt.

Harriet was known to carry a gun during her many trips back into Maryland to rescue family and friends from slavery. Over eleven years, Harriet succeeded in rescuing over 70 slaves during about thirteen such trips. Using strategic alliances, courage, and true wit Harriet managed to evade capture and detection, and as she said "I never lost a passenger, and I never run my train off the track."

Harriet showed true courage in the face of severe adversity. A slave had no rights. Slaves were not even considered to be human. They were considered property, and treated as such. So to stand up to an institution that was designed to hold you back and keep you down showed true bravery. Harriet was not afraid to stand up for her God-given rights, and the rights of all the other suffering slaves at the time. She carried God in her heart, and a gun on her hip. And she was not afraid to use either.

In April 2016, the U.S. Treasury Department announced that Harriet Tubman would replace Andrew Jackson on the center of a new $20 bill. Harriet Tubman has become widely-known and a well-respected American icon because of her bravery. Her legacy lives on.

Bessie Coleman

Bessie Coleman (January 26, 1892 to April 30, 1926) was an American aviator and the first black woman to earn a pilot's license. Bessie had a goal of being a pilot but because the schools in America would not permit blacks to attend, she decided to study French and go to France to study aviation at the well-known Caudron Brother's School of Aviation.

Bessie was born in Atlanta, Texas, and soon joined her family in the cotton fields. She was one of 13 children to Susan and George Coleman, who were illiterate and the children of slaves.

In 1901, her father left the family in search of better job opportunities in Oklahoma when Bessie was just a child. Bessie's mother and two older brothers went to work to support the family. They did the best they could but they still struggled. All of the children would eventually contribute as soon as they were old enough.

After receiving her pilot's license on June 15, 1921, Bessie traveled Europe, gaining further flying experience so that she could perform in air shows. Bessie would only agree to perform in these shows if the crowd was desegregated and all were permitted to enter through the same gates. Her goal was to start a flying school in America for African Americans. Bessie toured the country barnstorming, parachute jumping, and giving lectures to raise money for her African-American flying school.

Bessie's education consisted of completing all eight grades of her one-room school in Texas, then after saving up some money, she took her savings and enrolled in the Colored Agricultural and Normal University in Langston, Oklahoma. She completed only one term before running out of money.

Bessie was tragically killed in a freak accident when she was flying as a passenger in a plane she'd just purchased, with her mechanic manning the flight. Her seatbelt was not secure because Bessie was leaning over the side of the plane to survey the landscape in order to pick the best spot for her upcoming exhibition show.

The plane, which was worn, and poorly maintained, dived at an altitude of 1,000 feet then flipped over, throwing Bessie out. Moments later, her mechanic crashed. Both were killed. Five thousand mourners attended a memorial service for Bessie in Orlando, Florida. An estimated 15,000 people paid their respects in Chicago – at the funeral of that little girl from Texas who dreamed of a better life as she picked cotton at the dawn of the 20th century.

Only after her death did Bessie Coleman receive the attention she deserved. Her dream of a flying school for African Americans became a reality when William J. Powell established the Bessie Coleman Aero Club in Los Angeles in 1929. As a result of being affiliated, educated or inspired directly or indirectly by the aero club, flyers like the Five Blackbirds, the Flying Hobos, The Tuskegee Airmen and others continued to make Bessie's dream a reality.

In 1931, the Challenger Pilots' Association of Chicago began an annual flyover at Chicago's Lincoln Cemetery to honor Bessie. In 1977, women pilots in Chicago established the Bessie Coleman Aviators Club. In 1995, the U.S. Postal Service issued a "Bessie Coleman" stamp commemorating "her singular accomplishment in becoming the world's first African American pilot and, by definition, an American legend."

Bessie Coleman was a black woman but she didn't let the racially-charged views people held of her stop her from achieving her goal of becoming a pilot. Bessie must have been saying to herself, "That has nothing to do with me," as she jumped over one hurdle after another. She didn't let the prevailing thoughts of the time define her, or stop her. We thank Bessie for her undying commitment to being who she always knew she was, and accomplishing the things she always knew she could accomplish. Her black skin and her limited education didn't stop her. And neither should they stop you. Walk through life with confidence, sure of who you are, and determined to achieve your dreams, no matter what.

Madam C.J. Walker

Madam C.J. Walker, born Sarah Breedlove, December 23, 1867, is a true American hero. Not just to black people and people of color, but to all people no matter your race or gender.

Madam C.J. Walker was a pioneering woman, entrepreneur, factory owner, social activist, philanthropist, and a woman who trained and empowered other women to be financially independent and self-sufficient.

In 1906, Madam Walker started a hair care products company when she started losing her hair from a skin ailment. As you can imagine, Madam Walker was devastated when her hair started falling out in clumps. During this time, many women found themselves suffering with a similar scalp ailment which caused their hair to fall out.

Devastated, Madame Walker started experimenting with different homemade concoctions and store-bought hair treatments that she would put on her hair to treat her scalp. She soon stumbled upon a remedy that she herself concocted that would heal her scalp and cause her hair to grow back full and thick.

As Madame Walker's hair started to grow back she wanted to share her wonderful discovery with other black women, so she started traveling from house-to-house demonstrating her secret hair formula on women, and selling these products.

Her business was an instant success. This was a great accomplishment for someone who was a lowly washerwoman. Madam C.J. Walker became one of the most successful and wealthiest African American women in the country. She made her fortune developing, selling, and successfully marketing her own line of beauty and hair products for African American women through her company, Madame C.J. Walker Manufacturing Company.

Madam Walker's only daughter, A'lelia, watched her mother struggle with hair loss and the search for and the finding of a cure for her scalp ailment, and soon joined her mother in the company.

Madam Walker (Sarah Breedlove) was one of six children born to Owen and Minerva Breedlove in Delta, Louisiana. Born after the Emancipation Proclamation was signed, Madam Walker (Sarah) was the only child of her parents' born into freedom. The family had been owned by Robert W. Burney on the Madison Parish plantation in Louisiana.

Orphaned at age seven when first her mother died, then her father, Sarah moved in with her older sister, Louvenia, and brother-in-law, Jesse Powell at age 10. Madam Walker (Sarah) would later recount being mistreated by her sister's husband. Possibly to escape the abuse, she married Moses McWilliams in 1882, at age 14. Madam Walker (Sarah) and Moses had one daughter, Lelia McWilliams (she would eventually change her name to A'lelia), born on June 6, 1885.

She would marry again to Charles Joseph Walker, in 1906, after her first husband, Moses, died. The couple divorced in 1912, but throughout her marriage Sarah became known as Madam C.J. Walker.

In 1910, Madam Walker established the headquarters for the Madam C.J. Walker Manufacturing Company. She built a factory, hair salon, and beauty school to train her sales agents, and eventually added a laboratory to help with research.

Madam Walker believed in empowering women in business, and to be financially independent. Therefore, many of her employees, including those in key management and staff positions, were women. Madam C.J. Walker's company trained 20,000 women in beauty and hair care, and sales and marketing.

Madam Walker was a vocal activist and philanthropist, donating and helping to raise money for many worthy causes: YMCA, Tuskegee

Institute, Bethel African Methodist Episcopal Church, Indianapolis' Flanner House, and others.

When Madam C.J. Walker died on May 25, 1919 from kidney failure at age 51, she was a highly successful and wealthy woman. She was a self-made millionaire. She had built her business from the ground up into a major beauty and hair care empire. She helped scores of women achieve financial independence.

Madam Walker's story has inspired, and continues to inspire, generations of people. Her legacy lives on. Black when it was not popular, Madam Walker defined her own rules for success. She didn't let anyone else define her, or stop her from achieving her goals. Madam Walker was quoted as saying, "I had to make my own living, and my own opportunity." "I got my start by giving myself a start." "I am a woman who came from the cotton fields of the South. From there I was promoted to the washtub. From there I was promoted to the cook kitchen. And from there I promoted myself into the business of manufacturing hair goods and preparations. I have built my own factory on my own ground."

Use Madam C.J. Walker's story as inspiration to create your own opportunities, and make your own way. Madam Walker was not afraid to be who she was, and neither should you.

For more information on Madam C.J. Walker, visit the official Madam C.J. Walker website, run by her great-great granddaughter, A'Lelia Bundles: http://www.madamcjwalker.com/.

Walk Like a White Man — Quotes

❝ *That has nothing to do with me.* ❞

❝ *Some people like to surround themselves with darkness.* ❞

❝ *I refuse to walk in that darkness.* ❞

❝ *I think the more we get acquainted with people and get to know them personally these stereotypes will become less engrained in our minds and hearts.* ❞

❝ *We are all God's creatures, and made in His image.* ❞

> *Fear is constricting and binding. Freedom is what you should desire.*

> *Whether you are a black man, a white man, a Hispanic man, or an Asian man just know that you all have a place in this world.*

> *Don't allow negative stereotypes to change who you are.*

> *Anyone can walk like a white man regardless of the color of his or her skin.*

> *Walking like a white man is not a cultural thing.*

❝ *It's an attitude. It's a belief. It's a mindset.* ❞

❝ *Don't let society's limited perspectives and perceptions define who you are,*

or dim your shine. ❞

Epilogue

I can remember living in an apartment once that I absolutely loved. I love peace and quiet, and love to keep my personal space calm and soothing. This refreshes me. When I first moved into this apartment, the building was mostly occupied with elderly people. So the building was pretty quiet, which suited me fine. As a writer and thinker, I find inspiration in the solitude. The back of my apartment overlooked a small pond where ducks and geese would gather daily to swim or just sit out in the sun. And so in this environment I was inspired to write. I started my first blog while living in this apartment, and wrote and self-published two books.

But suddenly my quiet space was disrupted when some of the elderly residents started moving out one by one and new families, with small children, started moving in. One family had a young son around 8 or 9 years old. And a second family had two small kids around 5 and 2 years old. When I first saw the family with the two small children moving into the apartment right next door to me my first thought was, "Uh oh." I had lived in an apartment prior to this where there were kids living in the apartment above me, and it was not pleasant. Incidentally, I only lasted in this apartment about four months. Kids are naturally more active and make a lot of noise. They can't help themselves. They have a lot of energy to burn, and need a lot of space to burn this energy naturally. So when I saw the family with the small kids move in I thought this can't be good for me. And it turned out I was right. It wasn't good.

My once quiet oasis paradise was almost immediately disrupted with kids running and stomping through the apartment, opening and slamming doors, sometimes until 10 or 11 pm. Incidentally, I wondered why these kids didn't have a bedtime. Who lets small children stay up until 10 or 11 pm? In addition to the noise, the mother used to set off the smoke alarm in their apartment regularly when she cooked. She seemed to always burn something when she prepared her meals. And to add insult to injury, she would open the door of their apartment, which was right next door to mine, into the hallway to air out the smoke and fumes from her burnt meal. So this putrid smell would always make its way into my apartment, invading my personal space. It was a nightmare.

I worked from home at the time as a writer

so throughout the day I would be disrupted while trying to write by kids running, jumping, and slamming doors. And for some reason the woman in the apartment on the other side of me (yes, I was sandwiched in between them) felt the need to start slamming cabinets and drawers whenever she was in the kitchen preparing her meals. So between the kids on the left, and the cabinet slammer on the right, I had had enough.

I was working on my second book at the time and needed to finish it as the approaching deadline for publication neared. But I found it harder to concentrate in my once quiet apartment any longer. It was frustrating. I felt the cabinet slammer was doing it intentionally. It felt intentional anyway. It must have been her way of venting her frustration because I noticed a pattern with her husband who appeared to be very controlling. He would leave for work each day, but she never left the apartment without him. He came home for lunch every day, and she would have a prepared meal waiting for him. It was probably a cultural thing, but he seemed very controlling where she was subservient to him. She must have been frustrated with her situation and because she couldn't take it out on him she took it out on me.

One day when coming home from church, I decided to park my car in a different part of the parking lot of the apartment complex, where it couldn't be seen from my apartment, and enter my building undetected so that my neighbors would think that I wasn't home. Well to my surprise, this scheme worked wonders. I had a much-needed peaceful reprieve from cabinet slammer. Although I heard her in her kitchen preparing her meal as usual, she did not slam the cabinets once. Can you believe this? This got my wheels to turning and I decided to continue to park my car out of visibility and slip in and out the back patio door whenever I needed to leave the apartment. (I lived in a second-floor apartment, by the way. So I had to climb stairs to get up to my back patio.) I discovered that when cabinet slammer didn't think anyone was home she had no need to slam cabinets. No one to frustrate, save your energy, right? This let me know that it *was* intentional.

This method of entering and leaving through the back door helped me finish up my book in relative peace and quiet and meet my deadline. And although my neighbors didn't know what I was doing, others, I'm sure, noticed me "sneaking" in and out of my apartment. The building I lived in was directly across from the office. So they had to see me sneaking around and wondered what I was doing. Well I did this for a few weeks until one day, to my surprise, I discovered a letter in my mailbox from the apartment complex saying that starting Monday (this was on a Friday) the back stairs leading up to our patios were going to be removed and the patios sealed off. What?! This caught me completely off guard. I don't know how long this letter had been sitting in my mailbox because I rarely checked it because I got the majority of my mail sent to a P.O. Box. I usually only got junk mail in my apartment mailbox. I don't know what made me check the mailbox on this Friday but I'm glad I did. And sure enough, bright and early on Monday morning there was a demolition crew at our building to tear down the stairs leading up to the patios of the apartments in our building. And can you guess whose stairs were the first to go? You guessed it... mine.

Can you imagine if I had left out on Monday morning as usual for my daily walk, not knowing anything about the letter and the demolition of the patio stairs, with my front door barred (as I always barred it shut when I was in my apartment) to come home to find the stairs leading up to my apartment gone? There is no way I would have been able to get back into my apartment through the front door with it barred. I would have probably had to have used one of the demolition crew's ladders to get back into the apartment to unbar the door. How might that have gone? "Um, excuse me Mr. Construction Worker, do you mind if I borrow your ladder to climb up to my patio to get back into my apartment? I seem to have locked myself out." Oh yeah, that probably wouldn't have gone over too well. And they probably would have called the police.

Needless to say, I was not happy about the removal of the stairs and having my back exit sealed off. Yes, because my peace and quiet would probably be over the minute cabinet slammer knew I was home. But also because I was afraid that my neighbor, who kept setting off the smoke alarm, would one day burn the building down, and I would not have an alternate escape route should the fire end up in the hallway. Because of this, I thought I should say something to the office. I thought I could plead my case. And because I am a writer, and because I like to document my discussions, I wrote them a letter asking them if they would reconsider removing the patio stairs.

But in the end, this was hopeless. They had already made up their minds. The patio stairs had to go. And down they went. So I had to start using my front door again to exit and enter the apartment. But by this time, I had made great headway with my book so I was able to meet my deadline for publishing the book. But what I didn't realize, until later, is what writing that letter (I'm assuming) did to the people in the office. I think they took my pleas the wrong way. This let me know, later on, that they had probably been watching me leave and enter the apartment through the back door and got suspicious. They never mentioned it to me but I suspected as much.

A short time after this it was time to renew my lease. When I got the renewal notification in the mail I noticed that they were raising my rent by $30. At this point I had had enough of the apartment, the noisy kids, cabinet slammer, and the burning food and I thought it might be time to pack up my things and leave. I started looking at other apartments in the area. And I even called the office in my apartment complex to see if they had another second floor two-bedroom apartment coming available anytime soon. They did not – or at least that's what they told me at the time. I'm still not sure if I believed them. They did, however, have a more expensive two-bedroom with attached garage coming available and would I like to see it? I said yes. So I made an appointment the next week to see the two-bedroom garage apartment.

Even though I could no longer use the back door of my apartment, I had still continued to park my car in a distant parking lot and walk to my apartment building and enter my apartment through the front door. And on the day of my appointment to see the garage apartment, I was running a little late from running my errands. So when I got home I just parked my car where I usually parked it and walked directly to the office to meet the lady to go see the apartment. When I walked through the office door, I immediately sensed something was wrong. I've always been like this. My discernment is usually pretty high, and I know when something's not right. As I was walking from my car to the office I happened to notice a police car sitting along the entrance to the apartment, next to a pond that backed up to another apartment complex. I noticed the police car as I walked by, thought it was strange, but thought no more about it. So when I went into the office I noticed one of the maintenance workers sitting at the dining room table they had set up in the office. He had his laptop set up on the table and appeared to be working there. The tension in the room was pretty thick. Somewhere deep down inside me I knew something was wrong, but I wasn't able to fully process it until later on that day when I was able to piece everything together.

We went to see the apartment and I told her that I would let her know if I decided I wanted to take it. The apartment they showed me was already rented out. But they had a similar unit coming available soon. But I knew when I was leaving that I wasn't willing to pay a small fortune for an apartment. And the garage apartments at this complex cost a small fortune.

Here's what I was able to piece together after I was able to process everything later on in my mind. For some reason the people in the office must have felt spooked by my letter pleading to keep my patio stairs (because remember, they were watching me "sneak" around) that somewhere deep inside of them they must have rationalized in their minds that I was angry (the angry black woman stereotype) about them removing my stairs and felt they should probably have someone there when I showed up for my apartment tour – hence the strange police car out front, and the maintenance worker "working" in the office. So these women in the office (and they were white) must have convinced themselves that I was a threat (imagine that) and would possibly do harm to them. Now this is just not in my nature. And this does not even come close to who I am. I'm not a violent person. But what this incident did for me was that it left *me* spooked. That these people could easily jump to this kind of conclusion... almost out of nowhere. I thought to myself... I've got to get out of here, these people are crazy.

When people have this kind of irrational fear,

they are dangerous. Here I come along, innocently, not knowing anything is wrong and these people have escalated their fears and called in the "Calvary" to protect them (I guess from this 5 feet 2 inches black girl). Now if I would have spoken too loudly or reached in my purse too fast these fearful white women could have pulled out a gun and shot me... because *they* perceived me as a threat, in their minds. Yeah, I thought ... these people are crazy. I need to get out of here.

Now remember I spoke earlier about the white woman with the over-protective dog I passed on the sidewalk. This woman probably had this same irrational fear that the white women in the office had when she saw me walking toward her on the sidewalk. Something inside her must have triggered every negative emotion she has about black people. And the dog, picking up on this, lunged at me to protect her.

I shared this story with you to make a point. And this goes back to what I said earlier. People have their own perceptions of you based on what's going on inside them. When they see you, every negative or positive emotion, or good or bad vibe, or whatever, goes off inside them like smoke flares. And they have a choice in that moment of what they want to do. Will they embrace the irrational fear, or see it for what it really is... irrational? Now some of this is good. Our instincts help to keep us safe, and help us react in times of danger. But some of what's going on inside of us is irrational. We need to be able to distinguish between the two.

As I said earlier, when someone has a negative, unsubstantiated, bigoted assumption of me, it usually doesn't have anything to do with me. It has everything to do with who they are, and what they believe to be true based on what's going on inside them.

Now I made my decision to vacate my apartment and not take any other apartments in that complex because I saw that the people in the office were crazy. Irrationally crazy, with bigoted assumptions. And because of this I felt they were a threat to my safety. I thought that the best thing I could do was to get out of there. So I did. I took this threat seriously.

We need, all of us, to sit down and evaluate all of the emotions and thoughts and attitudes that live inside us. We need to take an honest assessment of ourselves. Is there anything we need to work on? Are we adding to society's problems, or helping to fix them? Are we part of the problem, or part of the solution?

I pray that this book becomes part of the solution. That it causes all of us to do some deep self-assessments to search for truth inside of us. And please know that sometimes doing self-assessment can uncover some ugliness inside us that we didn't know was there or that we pretend doesn't exist inside us. Self-assessment is hard to do. We'd much rather assess everyone else and tell them what they're doing wrong. But turn the microscope on yourself and find out what lives inside of you. Only when we are truthful with ourselves can we improve ourselves.

Here's to each one of us becoming a better person, friend, neighbor, and contributing member of society. Be a better you so the world can become a better place for all of us to live in. And remember, "That has nothing to do with me."

NAYLA BOOK PUBLISHERS

Thank you for purchasing this book.

Check out our blog at:
https://walklikeawhiteman.com

WalK liKe a WhiTe MaN™ is an inspirational blog for women. Empowering women to walk boldly and confidently into your destiny.

Stop by our online store to purchase your favorite WalK liKe a WhiTe MaN ™ merchandise.

Other books by Jeanita Jinnah:

An Open Letter to the Church: On Faith, Holiness, and Being Full of the Holy Ghost

The Purpose of Man

Step Out of the Shadows (For Widows Only!!!)™

www.ingramcontent.com/pod-product-compliance
Lightning Source LLC
Chambersburg PA
CBHW020658300426
44112CB00007B/436